Four Corners of the Sky
Poems, Chants and Oratory

Selected by Theodore Clymer

Illustrated by Marc Brown

An Atlantic Monthly Press Book
Little, Brown and Company
BOSTON   TORONTO

TEXT COPYRIGHT © 1975 BY THEODORE CLYMER

ILLUSTRATIONS COPYRIGHT © 1975 BY MARC BROWN

ALL RIGHTS RESERVED. NO PART OF THIS BOOK MAY BE REPRODUCED IN ANY FORM OR BY ANY ELECTRONIC OR MECHANICAL MEANS IN-CLUDING INFORMATION STORAGE AND RETRIEVAL SYSTEMS WITHOUT PERMISSION IN WRITING FROM THE PUBLISHER, EXCEPT BY A REVIEWER WHO MAY QUOTE BRIEF PASSAGES IN A REVIEW.

FIRST EDITION

T 05/75

Library of Congress Cataloging in Publication Data

Main entry under title:

Four corners of the sky.

"An Atlantic Monthly Press book."
Poems.
Bibliography: p. 48.
SUMMARY: An anthology of traditional chants and oratory from many American Indian tribes.
1. Indian poetry — Translations into English. 2. American poetry — Translations from Indian languages.
[1. Indian poetry — Collections] I. Clymer, Theodore.
II. Brown, Marc Tolon.
PZ8.3.F817   897   75-8893
ISBN 0-316-14761-3

ATLANTIC-LITTLE, BROWN BOOKS
ARE PUBLISHED BY
LITTLE, BROWN AND COMPANY
IN ASSOCIATION WITH
THE ATLANTIC MONTHLY PRESS

Published simultaneously in Canada
by Little, Brown & Company (Canada) Limited

PRINTED IN THE UNITED STATES OF AMERICA

For Pat

FOUR CORNERS OF THE SKY is a celebration of life, a collection of songs, chants, and oratory of the American Indian. These poems were originally recorded from various tribes over a broad span of time and from a number of places. For many of these poems and chants we have clear information about their use and meaning; for others we can only guess. I am deeply indebted to the men and women who collected these oral traditions, allowing us to share the feelings—in good times and bad—of American Indians.

The wolves are howling.
Let this be a pleasant day.
—Clayoquot

The morning star is up.
I cross the mountains into the light of the sea.

— Papago

The bear stands.
I am telling this.
Yonder the bear stands.
He faces the east just before the sun appears.
Yonder the bear stands.
Now the sun is coming.

— Pawnee

At dawn the bear stood to the east, held up his front paws, and received the great power of the sun. The first rays carried the greatest strength.

What is this
I promise you?
The skies shall be bright and clear for you.
This is what I promise you.

— Chippewa

This is an initiation song for young men about to become full members of the warrior group.

Early this morning the coming of the sun,
For what purpose is it coming?
Perhaps for sons and daughters of the people it is coming.
    Yonder in the west,
    People, what do you think?
    What do you say? Shall we sit and sing?

—Isleta

An early morning song chanted by the women as they grind corn for the day's food.

The little blackbirds are singing this song
as they dance around the four corners of the sky.

—Yuma

Do not touch me!
There is nothing you can do,
You rattlesnake with your belly full,
Lying where the ground-squirrel holes are thick.
Do not touch me!
What can you do to me?
Rattlesnake in the tree clump,
Stretched in the shade,
You can do nothing.
Do not touch me!
Rattlesnake of the plains,
You whose white eye
The sun shines on,
Do not touch me!

—Yokut

Part of an elaborate ceremony, this chant is a warning to rattlesnakes. The shaman called the snakes from their dens, handled them, and even allowed himself to be bitten to protect the tribe.

What horse is trying to catch me?
    What horse is trying to catch me?
The horse with the star forehead
    Now slowly gains upon me.

We are sitting here together.
    We are sitting here together.
Singing the song of the east.
    Singing the song of the west.

                      —Pima

A playful song with which an Indian coaxes a wild horse to him and tames it.

I am the Grizzly Bear.
Don't pass me by when I lie eating.

                      —Tsimshian

Who is my equal or can compare with me?
I have forty whales on my beach.

—Makah

Comes the deer to my singing,
Comes the deer to my song,
Comes the deer to my singing.

From the Mountain Black,
From the summit,
Down the trail, coming, coming now,
Comes the deer to my singing.

Starting with his left fore-foot,
Stamping, turns the frightened deer,
Comes the deer to my singing.

Comes the deer to my singing,
Comes the deer to my song,
Comes the deer to my singing.

— Navajo

This is part of a much longer chant given to the Navahos by the God Hastyayalti. It was used to lure deer towards the hunter.

He is out of sight.
But I put my ear to a tree in the forest.
And that brings me the sound.
I hear when the moose makes his next leap.
I follow.

— Wabanaki

The heart of the mountain goat is broken when it falls below.

—Tsimshian

This song typifies the Indian's compassion for wild creatures.

Hanging motionless in the sky.
Yet terrible in its power to destroy.
—Papago

Nicely, nicely, nicely, nicely, there away in the east,
The rain clouds are caring for the little corn plants
As a mother takes care of her baby.
— Acoma

Nicely while it is raining,
Corn plant, I am singing for you.
Nicely while the water is streaming,
Vine plant, I am singing for you.
— Acoma

Let us go to the Indian village, said all the rain gods,
So that the people of the village will be happy again.
— Zuni

My great corn plants,
Among them I walk.
I speak to them;
They hold out their hands to me.

My great squash vines,
Among them I walk.
I speak to them;
They hold out their hands to me.

— Navajo

The Indian learned long before the white man that plants respond to prayers and affection.

My tail rattles,
My ears rattle,
Each end rattles.
My whole body rattles.
My face is striped.
My back is striped.

— Mandan

A children's game, this is the acting out of a folk tale about how Skunk and Coyote were chased from a village.

Sleep well,
Your mother has gone to get a long turtle,
Little boy, go to sleep,
That is what your mother said.
—Seminole

The "long turtle" may have been an alligator or the long-tailed turtle of the Florida swamps.

Puva, puva, puva,
In the trail the beetles
On each other's backs are sleeping,
So on mine, my baby, thou
Puva, puva, puva!
—Hopi

An old lullaby comparing a child on its mother's back to a beetle carried on the back of another beetle.

Gopher sees where the stone is,
Gopher sees where the stone is.
Strike on! Strike on!

— Navajo

A song for a gambling game in which several moccasins are buried with a stone hidden in one. A player guesses which moccasin holds the stone and strikes at it with a stick. Because the gopher digs beneath the earth, he knows where the stone is.

To the medicine man's house they have led me.
To the medicine man's house they have led me.
Inside the house they have brought me.
Elder Brother is there and owl feathers fly about.
The owl feathers sing in the air.

—Papago

The medicine man's house is filled with bundles, magic signs, and bits of fur, bone and bead strung on leather thongs. As the patient enters, he is suddenly blinded by a swirling mass of owl feathers, powerful omens of good.

I know everything in the bottom of my heart.
From Coyote I learn all this.
I get it and keep it within me, and hold it there.

— Papago

Coyote was the giver of all wisdom. Here the shaman brags that he has retained all the coyote has taught him. Therefore, he is a great medicine man.

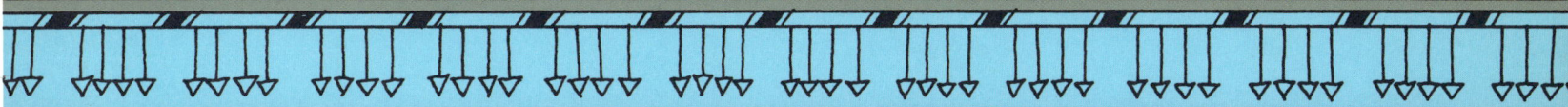

Haih! the white bird of omen,
He flies around the clouds and skies—
Around the clouds and skies—
By his bright eyes I see—I see—I know.

— Chippewa

I am rising to seek the war-path.
The earth and the sky are before me.
I walk by day and by night.
And the evening star is my guide.

— Chippewa

I am going to be a great warrior.
The crows have given me medicine to make me so.

— Clayoquot

A crow's wing or perhaps a single feather gives power to the singer. He may have been given the shaman's bundle, containing a crow feather.

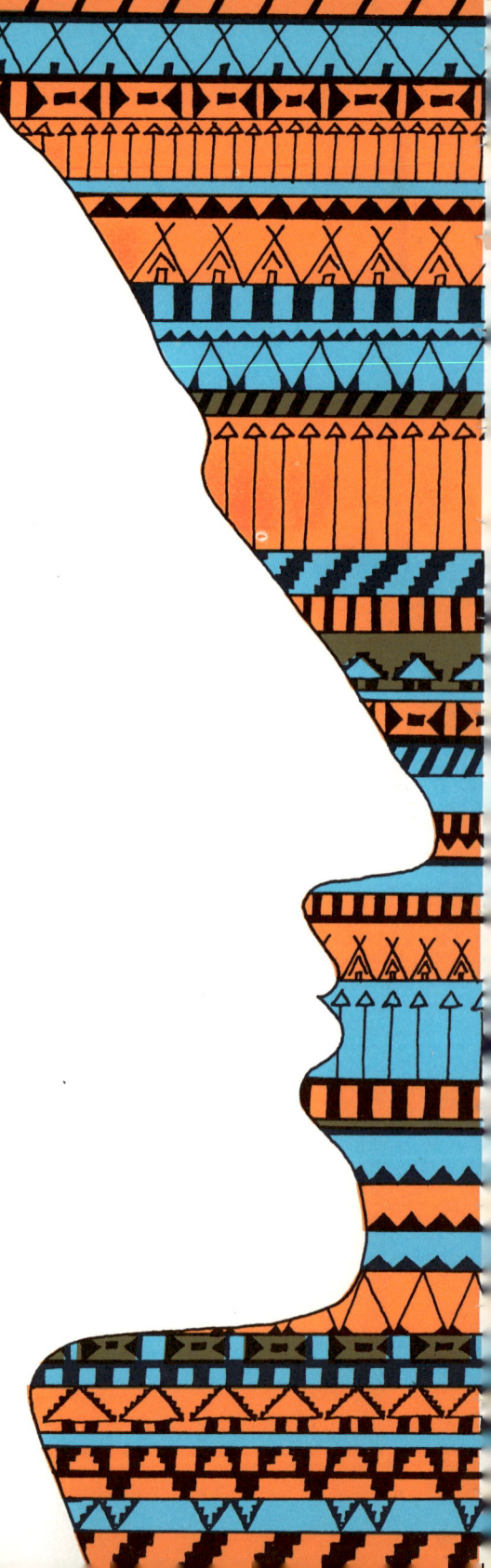

Friends,
The many lands
You fear.
In them without fear I have walked.
The black face-paint
I seek.

— Sioux

The brave who first "counted coup" was permitted to blacken his face as a reward for his bravery.

You will always find me
By the beating of my drum.

— Makah

The singer is blind and he calls out to any who may hear his drum.

And here, on my breast, have I bled!
See — see! My battle-scars!
Ye mountains, tremble at my yell!
I strike for life.
              — Chippewa

A soldier
I am.
It is but a short life
I have to live.
          —Sioux

Crow Indian,
You must watch your horses.
A horse thief
Often
Am I.

—Sioux

The greatest measure of wealth for Plains Indians was the horse. This is a playful song — and a warning.

A Lone Wolf I am…
I roam in many places…
I am weary.

—Sioux

My people are few.
They resemble the scattering trees
of a storm-swept plain.

—Salish

From a treaty speech by Chief Seattle, 1855.

The water bug is dipping
the end of his long body in the water
and dancing up and down.
—Yuma

Downy white feathers are moving beneath the sunset
And along the edge of the world.
—Papago

How shall I begin my song
In the blue night that is settling?
I will sit here and begin my song.
—Papago

The light glow of evening,
   The light glow of evening
Comes as the quails fly slowly,
   And it settles on the young.
          —Pima

The quail in the bush is making his whirring.
          —Yaqui

The evening glow yet lingers,
    The evening glow yet lingers,
And I sit with my gourd rattle
    Engaged in the sacred chant.
As I wave the eagle feathers
    We hear the magic sounding.

—Pima

A cure chanted by the medicine man.

Brown owls come here in the blue evening,
They are hooting about,
They are shaking their wings and hooting.
— Papago

The owl is sacred, much feared and the source of cures.

That wind, that wind
Shakes my tipi, shakes my tipi,
And sings a song for me.
— Kiowa

The night bat
Rising flies.
I tell it.
I sing it.
— Mojave

A dream is the source of this song.

What is life?
It is the flash of a firefly in the night.
It is the breath of a buffalo in the wintertime.
It is the little shadow which runs across the grass
 and loses itself in the sunset.

— Blackfoot

A deathbed statement attributed to Crowfoot, a Canadian Indian chief.

I am simply on the earth.
Need I be afraid?

— Hidatsa

You are like a friend of mine.
I think we are brothers.

— Cherokee

Toward calm and shady places
I am walking
On the earth.

—Chippewa

This cure chant could be sung only by those who bought it from the medicine man.

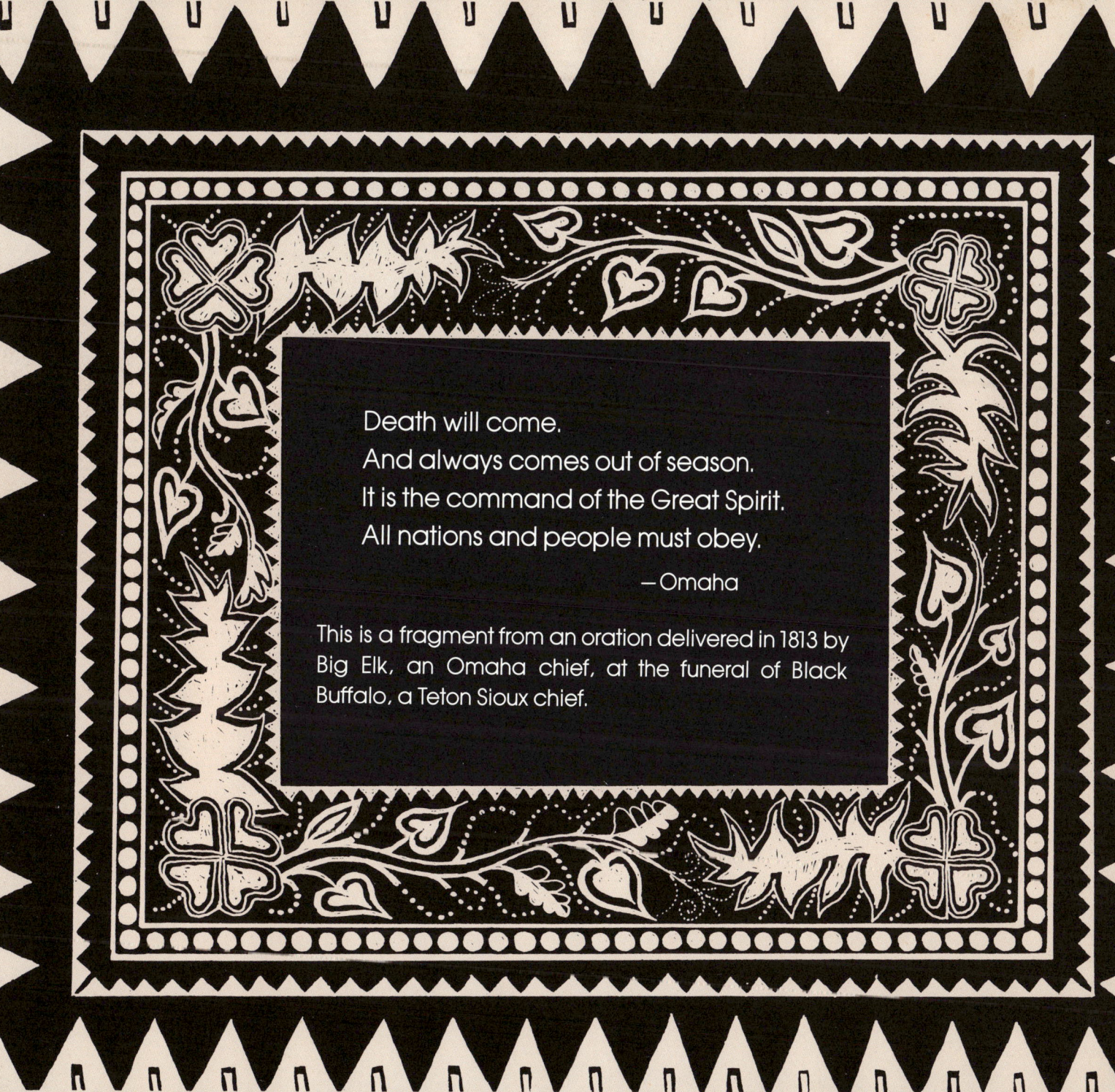

From the middle
Of the great water
I am called
By the spirit.
　　—Chippewa

The stones are all that last long.
　　　　　—Cheyenne

Raven,
I am going to die.
Fly away.
　　—Mandan

The raven's repeated call was a sign of death.

In old age,
The beautiful trail
May I walk.

— Navajo

When the Indians were forced upon reservations they created the Ghost Dance Religion, which promised a return to the good life of earlier times. Great gatherings celebrated the coming of a messiah. These four songs grew out of this religion.

Father, have pity on me.
Father, have pity on me.
I am crying for thirst.
I am crying for thirst.
All is gone…I have nothing to eat.
All is gone…I have nothing to eat.
— Arapaho

My son, let me grasp your hand,
Says the father.
You shall live,
You shall live,
Says the father.
I bring you a pipe,
Says the father.
By means of it you shall live,
By means of it you shall live,
Says the father.

—Sioux

I circle around
The boundaries of the earth —
Wearing the long wing feathers as I fly.
— Arapaho

Bibliography

Bradbury, John. *Travels in the Interior of America,* 2nd ed. London: Sherwood, Neely, and Jones, 1819, p. 228.

Curtis, Natalie, ed. *The Indians' Book.* New York: Dover Publications, 1907, pp. 11, 370, 480.

Densmore, Frances. "Cheyenne and Arapaho Music." Southwest Museum Papers, No. 10. Los Angeles: Southwest Museum, 1936, p. 35.

———. "Chippewa Music." Smithsonian Institution, U.S. Bureau of American Ethnology, Bulletin 45. Washington: U.S. Government Printing Office, 1910, pp. 82, 110.

———. "Chippewa Music—II." Smithsonian Institution, U.S. Bureau of American Ethnology, Bulletin 53. Washington: U.S. Government Printing Office, 1913, pp. 125, 231.

———. "Mandan and Hidatsa Music." Smithsonian Institution, U.S. Bureau of American Ethnology, Bulletin 80. Washington: U.S. Government Printing Office, 1923, pp. 49, 93, 121.

———. "Music of Acoma, Isleta, Cochiti and Zuñi Pueblos." Smithsonian Institution, U.S. Bureau of American Ethnology, Bulletin 165. Washington: U.S. Government Printing Office, 1957, pp. 33, 48, 62, 100.

———. "Nootka and Quileute Music." Smithsonian Institution, U.S. Bureau of American Ethnology, Bulletin 124. Washington: U.S. Government Printing Office, 1939, pp. 117, 185, 199, 225.

———. "Papago Music." Smithsonian Institution, U.S. Bureau of American Ethnology, Bulletin 90. Washington: U.S. Government Printing Office, 1929, pp. 27, 70, 95, 105, 117, 118, 133.

———. "Pawnee Music." Smithsonian Institution, U.S. Bureau of American Ethnology, Bulletin 93. Washington: U.S. Government Printing Office, 1929, p. 39.

———. "Seminole Music." Smithsonian Institution, U.S. Bureau of American Ethnology, Bulletin 161. Washington: U.S. Government Printing Office, 1956, p. 204.

———. "Teton Sioux Music." Smithsonian Institution, U.S. Bureau of American Ethnology, Bulletin 61. Washington: U.S. Government Printing Office, 1918, pp. 109, 337, 454.

———. "Yuman and Yaqui Music." Smithsonian Institution, U.S. Bureau of American Ethnology, Bulletin 110. Washington: U.S. Government Printing Office, 1932, pp. 133, 146, 157.

Garfield, Viola, Paul Wingert, and Marius Barbeau. "The Tsimschian: Their Arts and Music." Publications of the American Ethnological Society, *18,* ed. Marian W. Smith. New York: J. J. Augustin, 1951, pp. 129, 144.

Kroeber, A. L., "Handbook of the Indians of California." Smithsonian Institution, U.S. Bureau of American Ethnology, Bulletin 78. Washington: U.S. Government Printing Office, 1925, pp. 506, 758.

Matthews, Washington. "Navajo Gambling Songs." *American Anthropologist,* Washington: American Anthropological Society, 2, 1889, p. 11.

———. "The Night Chant, A Navajo Ceremony." In *Memoirs of the American Museum of Natural History.* New York: The American Museum of Natural History, 6, 1902, pp. 112, 293.

Monture, Ethel Brant. *Canadian Portraits: Brant, Crowfoot and Oronhyatekha, Famous Indians.* Toronto: Clarke, Irwin and Co., 1960, p. 128.

Mooney, John. "The Ghost-Dance Religion." In *The Fourteenth Annual Report of the Bureau of Ethnology, 1892-1893.* Washington: U.S. Government Printing Office, 1896, pp. 970, 977, 1062, 1072, 1089.

Russell, Frank. "The Pima Indians." In *The Twenty-sixth Annual Report of the United States Bureau of American Ethnology, 1904-1905.* Washington: U.S. Government Printing Office, 1908, pp. 302, 318.

Schoolcraft, Henry, LL.D. *Historical and Statistical Information Respecting the History, Condition and Prospects of the Indian Tribes of the United States: Collected and Prepared under the Direction of the Bureau of Indian Affairs,* Part I. Philadelphia: Lippincott, Grambo and Co., 1851, pp. 399, 402.

———. *Information Respecting the History, Condition and Prospects of the Indian Tribes of the United States: Collected and Prepared under the Direction of the Bureau of Indian Affairs,* Part II. Philadelphia: Lippincott, Grambo and Co., 1852, p. 61.

———. *Information Respecting the History, Condition and Prospects of the Indian Tribes of the United States: Collected and Prepared under the Direction of the Bureau of Indian Affairs,* Part V. Philadelphia: Lippincott, Grambo and Co., 1855, p. 564.

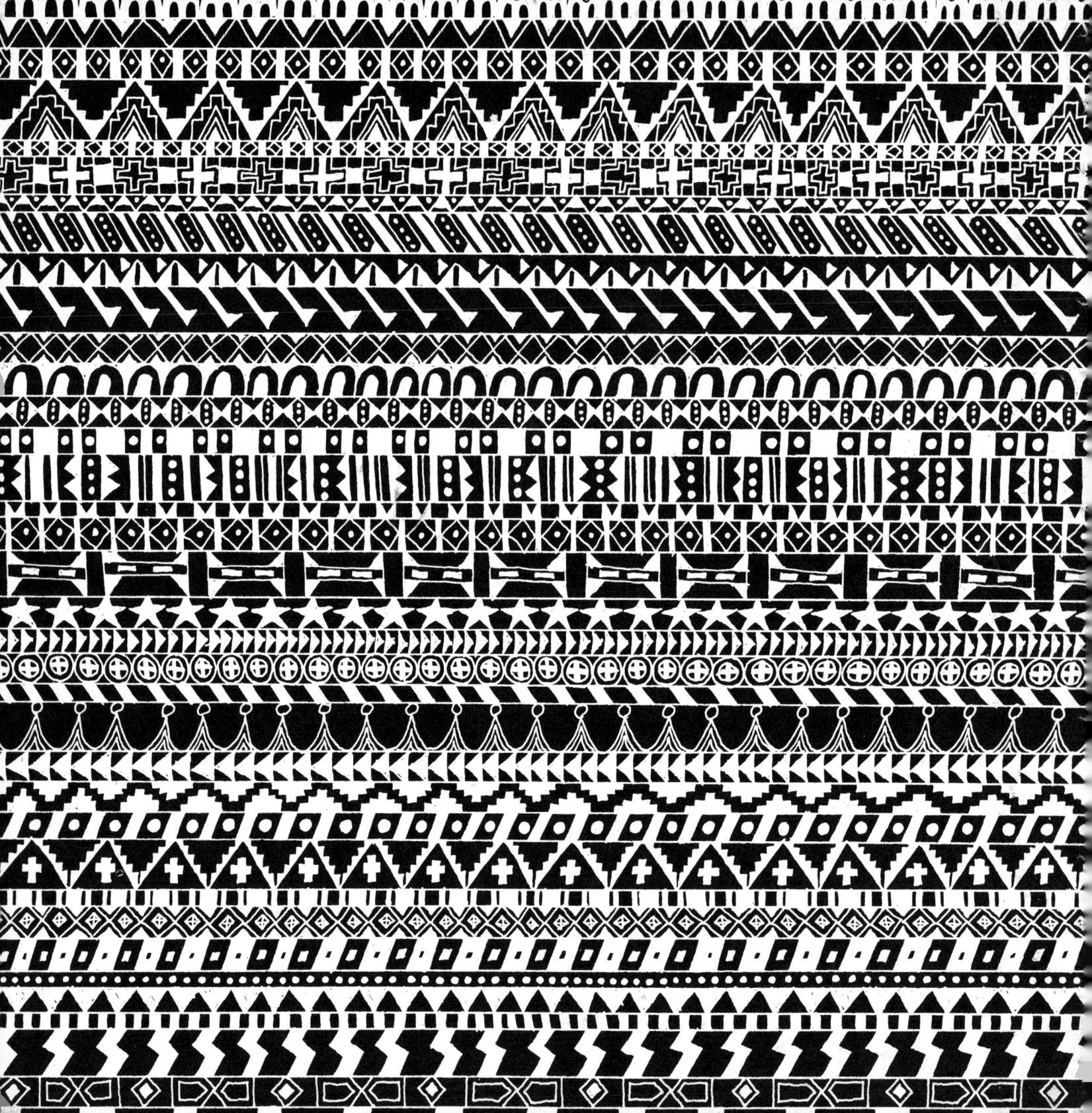